ABORTION IS GOOD

--FOR AMERICA

--AND THE WORLD

WHY THE OPPOSITION?

Dr. Bob O'Connor

Total Health Publications

2019

RECENT BOOKS BY DR. O'CONNOR

Let's Look at Our Democracy

Make America Great—Like Norway

Abortion—Dissecting the Old and
NEW Arguments

LOVE—The You, The Me, The Us

Table of Contents

CHAPTER ONE 4
WHY THE OPPOSITION TO ABORTION IN THE UNITED 4
STATES? 4
  TRADITION 4
  TRADITIONS, RELIGIOUS BELIEFS, AND EDUCATION 4
CHAPTER TWO 6
WHAT DOES THE BIBLE SAY? 6
  LIFE STARTS WITH THE FIRST BREATH 6
  ABORTION IS REQUIRED IN THE BIBLE IN AT LEAST ONE 6
  CIRCUMSTANCE 6
    THE FETUS NOT A PERSON—AND IS NOT SACRED 7
  A FETUS IS NOT YET A PERSON—ONLY THE PROPERTY OF THE 7
  HUSBAND 7
    GOD IS NOT PRO-LIFE 8
  SHOULD CHRISTIAN ADVOCATES SPEND MORE TIME ADVOCATING WHAT
  THE BIBLE HAS ACTUALLY APPROVED? 9
    SLAVERY 9
    CAPITAL PUNISHMENT 10
    ADVOCATING THE APPROVED PRACTICES OF THE BIBLE 10
  AND ANOTHER THEOLOGICAL QUESTION! 10
CHAPTER THREE 12
WHAT DOES FEDERAL LAW SAY? 12
    RELIGIOUS ADVOCATES FOR CHANGING THE LAW 13
CHAPTER FOUR 14
OPINIONS, FACTS, AND EFFECTIVE THINKING 14
  HOW MUCH DO WE EVALUATE THE ISSUES? 14
    DO WE REALLY NEED MORE LABORERS? 15
  AND WHAT ABOUT THE PLANET'S MAJOR PROBLEM-- 15
  OVERPOPULATION? 15
  INTERNATIONAL HUMAN RIGHTS STATEMENTS 16
    RELIGIOUS BELIEFS CAN INTERFERE WITH SOCIAL REALITIES 16
    DECLARATIONS OF HUMAN RIGHTS 16
    WHAT DO THE LATEST ABORTION LAWS PROTECT? 17
    PENALTIES FOR THOSE WHO AID IN ABORTIONS 18
  DOES EDUCATION, OR THE LACK OF IT, PLAY A PART? 19
    YOUNG UNEDUCATED MOTHERS IN ALABAMA 20
    WHO IS RIGHT ON THIS ISSUE OF ABORTION? 20
    IT IS ABOUT TRADITION 20
    BUT NEW LAWS CHANGE OUR TRADITIONS 20
CHAPTER FIVE 22
POSITIVES FOR SOCIETY 22
    FINANCIAL REASONS 23
  FEWER PEOPLE WILL REDUCE THE GREENHOUSE GASES THAT CREATE
  GLOBAL WARMING AND CLIMATE CHANGE 25
    FEWER PEOPLE EASES THE NEED FOR FRESH WATER FOR PERSONAL
    NEEDS AND FOOD PRODUCTION 25
    FREEDOM FOR THE CITIZENS TO CHOSE THE WAY TO LIVE THEIR LIVES
   26
    SEPARATION OF CHURCH AND STATE 26
    OUR FREEDOM OF SPEECH IDEAS 27
  AND BACK TO ABORTION 28
APPENDIX A   ABORTION INFORMATION 29
INDEX 30

CHAPTER ONE

WHY THE OPPOSITION TO ABORTION IN THE UNITED STATES?

TRADITION

What we learned at mother's knee—or some other joint, is fundamental to our belief system. We seldom think our way into our beliefs, we merely accept what we have been told by our parents, priests, and neighbors.

Traditions can be valuable, like looking both ways before you cross a street. But they can also be counterproductive, like protecting coal mining when there are cheaper and cleaner methods of producing electricity.

Abortion is not proscribed in the Bible. In fact, it is quite clear that life begins with the first breath—not at conception or with the first heartbeat! The Jews, because they read the Scriptures, are well aware of this fact. According to Religion News Service, in a survey done in 2016, only 20% of Christians had read the whole Bible, while over 50% had not read any part, or had read only a few stories.

Still, the United States is apparently a very religious country. In an international survey measuring the importance of religion in one's everyday life, 70%believed that religion was important in their lived. This compared with Estonia, the Scandinavian countries, and most of Europe which were significantly less religious. These less religious countries had only 15 to 20% of their populations that found religion important in their lives. At the other end of the scale, Somalia, Bangladesh, and Ethiopia had 100% of their populations who believed deeply in their religions.

TRADITIONS, RELIGIOUS BELIEFS, AND EDUCATION

Traditions are like matter, which according to Newton's laws of motion, remains at rest until moved. When moved, an equal and opposite force is exerted against the moving force. From an intellectual point of view, we can expect opposition to the long-held view that abortion is illegal, because at the beginning of the 20th century abortion was outlawed in most countries.

Historically, religion sanctifies what society is already doing. When Moses descended Mt. Sinai with his Ten Commandments, society had already decided that murder, stealing, adultery, and bearing false witness were bad for society, and that there was a god above the society. The Babylonian king, Hammurabi, had already spelled it out, in far more detail, a thousand years earlier.

So, looking at the needs of American society 100 years ago we can see how abortion might not be desirable—so this societal need might be championed by the various religions.

At that time, in 1900, the life expectancy for men was 41. We were in a period where the economic system was based on physical labor. Today, by contrast, the male life expectancy is 79 and the economic system is highly intellectually intensive—so the worker can work more years. Consequently, we don't need as many workers. And those we need require much more education. Also, few women worked in 1900, today most women do. Additionally, computers, robotics, 3d printing, and artificial intelligence make every worker more productive.

As the methods of aborting have become incredibly safe, abortion is much safer than giving birth. The freedom of women to attend universities and to enter the labor force gives women more choice in choosing relationships and motherhood. This has been very important in reversing traditions in most of the Western world. 98% of countries allow abortion to save the life of the mother. 63% of countries allow it to preserve the mental health pf the pregnant woman. 43% allow it in the case of rape or incest. 39% allow it if the infant is to be severely impaired. 33% allow abortion for economic or social reasons. 27% allow it when requested by the woman.

The developing countries are much less likely to allow abortions than are the developed countries.

CHAPTER TWO

WHAT DOES THE BIBLE SAY?

A Pew report, surveying over 35,000 people found that 45% of Christians seldom or never read the Bible, but 35% read it at least once a week. The sects with the highest level of readers were: Jehovah's Witnesses, Mormons, Evangelicals, and the historically Black Protestants. These were in the 60 to 85% ranges. Catholics and mainline Protestants were 30% or less. It might also be noted that the less the educational level, the more likely that the person would be: a Bible-reader, believe that it was the word of God, and that abortion and homosexuality should be prohibited.

The survey did not indicate whether the Bible was read in its entirety or whether it was understood-- or whether the beliefs of the readers came from their ministers and priests.

If people have read and understood the Bible, these following citations will not be new, but for those who believe that the Bible is the word of God, and literally true, these passages should be internalized when deciding on a religious proscription against abortion.

LIFE STARTS WITH THE FIRST BREATH

The Bible is generally clear that life starts with the first breath. The Jewish tradition has followed this idea since it was introduced. Jeremiah did enunciate a contrary view, but it was definitely a minority view, compared to the writings of Moses. In Genesis 2:7 it is written that, "Then the LORD God formed man of dust from the ground, and breathed into his nostrils the breath of life; and man became a living being."

ABORTION IS REQUIRED IN THE BIBLE IN AT LEAST ONE CIRCUMSTANCE

In Numbers 5:11, the Lord spoke to Moses about what should be the priest's duty when a woman has been accused of adultery. She is given "bitter water" to cause an abortion. In verses 21 and 22 it says when the priest is to put the woman under this curse—"may the LORD cause you to become a curse among your people when he makes your womb miscarry and your abdomen swell. May this water that brings a curse enter your body so that your abdomen swells or your womb miscarries." So, according to what God told Moses, abortion is required of a woman is pregnant from an adulterous relationship. In fact, it is part of the "curse" of her misdeed.

American laws that disallow abortions for rape, incest, and adultery would seem to be diametrically opposed to what God told Moses.

On the other hand, nowhere does the Bible say that it is not allowed in cases where it is voluntary. As Moses mentioned, there was at least one abortifacient that was known in those early times.

Hosea (9:14) tells us that part of the punishment for not being faithful to the God of Israel is that "wombs that miscarry and breasts that are dry." So God will cause the spontaneous abortions.

THE FETUS NOT A PERSON—AND IS NOT SACRED

In Deuteronomy 28:18, God warns the Israelites that they must keep his Commandments. He cites the benefits of following them and the evils of disobedience. Among the evils are that: "The fruit of your womb will be cursed, and the crops of your land, and the calves of your herds and the lambs of your flocks.

Ripping open pregnant women is allowed by God for disobedience to Him, but it is also prevalent in wars, which He could control if He so desired.

God will punish the Israelites by destroying their unborn children, who will die at birth, or perish in the womb, or never even be conceived. (Hosea 9:10-16)

Even Jesus, in commenting on the approaching end of the world, thought not of sparing pregnant or nursing women. In Matthew 24:19 he said, "Woe to pregnant women and those who are nursing." So the often merciless God of the Old Testament may not be dead!

A FETUS IS NOT YET A PERSON—ONLY THE PROPERTY OF THE HUSBAND

EXODUS 21:22-25 "If people are fighting and hit a pregnant woman and she gives birth prematurely but there is no serious injury, the offender must be fined whatever the woman's husband demands and the court allows. But if there is serious injury, you are to take life for life, eye for eye, tooth for tooth, hand for hand, foot for foot, burn for burn, wound for wound, bruise for bruise."

GOD IS NOT PRO-LIFE

The killing of all people, including fetuses and children in Sodom and Gomorrah, is but one of about two dozen of such God caused mass extinctions. God certainly directed David's shot that killed Goliath. And in Jeremiah 44:7-8 It is said about worshipping other gods: "Now this is what the LORD God Almighty, the God of Israel, says: Why bring such great disaster on yourselves by cutting off from Judah the men and women, the children and infants, and so leave yourselves without a remnant? Why arouse my anger with what your hands have made . . ."

In 2 Samuel 11, we have the account of David seeing the beautiful Bathsheba, whom he had been told was married. He slept with her in an adulterous affair and she became pregnant. So David put her husband, Uriah, in the front of the ranks where he was certain to be killed—and he was. (Verses 14-17) Then Bathsheba became David's wife. So David was involved in an adulterous affair-- a capital crime. "If a man commits adultery with another man's wife—with the wife of his neighbor—both the adulterer and the adulteress are to be put to death." (Leviticus 20:10) It is echoed in Deuteronomy 22:22, "If a man is found sleeping with another man's wife, both the man who slept with her and the woman must die. You must purge the evil from Israel."

And it might be said that David planned the killing of Uriah. 2 Samuel 11:27, but that conspiracy is not clearly a Biblical sin, as it is in federal law where conspiracy to commit murder can bring up to life imprisonment.

Still, we are told that "the Lord was displeased with him." Perhaps it is like today where crimes by people in high places are not as severely punished as those committed by people farther down the pecking order!

One would expect that because of the Israelites enslavement in Egypt, that the message of the Bible would be totally anti-slavery. However, one finds strong pro-and anti-slavery positions in both the Old and the New testaments. A few of the many references follow:

Leviticus 25:44-46--"As for your male and female slaves whom you may have: you may buy male and female slaves from among the nations that are around you. You may also buy from among the strangers who sojourn with you and their clans that are with you, who have been born in your land, and they may be your property. You may bequeath them to your sons after you to inherit as a possession forever. You may make slaves of them, but over your brothers the people of Israel you shall not rule, one over another ruthlessly."

Exodus 21:20-21 --"If a man strikes his slave, male or female, with a rod and the slave dies under his hand, he shall be avenged. But if the slave survives a day or two, he is not to be avenged, for the slave is his money."

Exodus 21:26-27 --"When a man strikes the eye of his slave, male or female, and destroys it, he shall let the slave go free because of his eye. If he knocks out the tooth of his slave, male or female, he shall let the slave go free because of his tooth."

Exodus 21:2 --"When you buy a Hebrew slave, he shall serve six years, and in the seventh he shall go out free, for nothing."

And from the new Testament:

Colossians 4:1 --"Masters, treat your slaves justly and fairly, knowing that you also have a Master in heaven."

Ephesians 6:5 –"Slaves, obey your earthly masters with fear and trembling, with a sincere heart, as you would Christ,"

Titus 2:9-10 –"Slaves are to be submissive to their own masters in everything; they are to be well-pleasing, not argumentative, not pilfering, but showing all good faith, so that in everything they may adorn the doctrine of God our Savior."

1 Timothy 6:1-2 "Let all who are under a yoke as slaves regard their own masters as worthy of all honor, so that the name of God and the teaching

maynot be reviled. Those who have believing masters must not be disrespectful on the ground that they are brothers; rather they must serve all the better since those who benefit by their good service are believers and beloved. Teach and urge these things."

CAPITAL PUNISHMENT

The worst offense in the Bible is worshipping a false god. This is mentioned over 300 times and it carried the death penalty. Blasphemy is a similarly nasty offense. Adultery is sometimes a capital offense (Leviticus 20:10), as is murder (Leviticus 24:17) and sometimes rape.

ADVOCATING THE APPROVED PRACTICES OF THE BIBLE

It would appear that if the message of the Bible is primary in some people's lives, that they should spend their time advocating and legislating for propositions actually found in the Bible—such as advocating slavery and capital punishment.

The anti-abortion legislatures tend to be for capital punishment for murder, as the Bible teaches. But perhaps they should also work to legislate capital punishment for blasphemy and adultery. We might assume that there are too many people shouting "Jesus Christ" when they are angry at things, or "God damn you" when they are angry at people. Shouldn't they be stoned?

As long as we have a nominal separation of church and state it would be unwise to seek to reinstall slavery as an economic tool. In fact, it isn't needed now with automation, artificial intelligence, robots, and 3D printing. And, of course, it would require a Constitutional amendment to invalidate the 13th Amendment.

AND ANOTHER THEOLOGICAL QUESTION!

Anti-abortion zealots assert that human life begins at conception, and therefore the fertilized egg possesses all constitutional rights of a living person. It follows that destruction of a conceived embryo (blastocyst) is murder. This is the basis for the "personhood" argument which has been defeated in five statewide initiatives since 2010.

The Bible declares that God breathed life into man's body (Genesis 2:7). At least a dozen more verses indicate that breath is synonymous with life. This scriptural truth completely contradicts the personhood dogma.

More importantly, if the fertilized ovum is a person, as anti-abortion extremists claim, then God's record as the greatest murderer of unborn children is expanded further. That is because most fertilized eggs either fail to implant in the uterine wall and pass out of the body, or they do implant, begin to develop and then are spontaneously aborted. Fewer than one-third of fertilized ova survive to become living humans.

Why does God murder untold millions of these "persons" every year in the U.S. alone? Why did God, who allegedly loves the unborn and hates abortion, kill so many unborn children, adolescents and adults throughout biblical history? Why do fundamentalists pursue a political agenda that is thoroughly refuted by God's word?

CHAPTER THREE

WHAT DOES FEDERAL LAW SAY?

Aborting an embryo or fetus is not killing a person under Federal law. In the Unborn Victims of Violence Act of 2004, abortion is specifically excluded.

An embryo or fetus does not have rights under Federal law.

> As used in this chapter, the term "United States person" means any United States citizen or alien admitted for permanent residence in the United States, and any corporation, partnership, or other organization organized under the laws of the United States.
> a) In determining the meaning of any Act of Congress, or of any ruling, regulation, or interpretation of the various administrative bureaus and agencies of the United States, the words "person", "human being", "child", and "individual", shall include every infant member of the species homo sapiens who is born alive at any stage of development.
> (b) As used in this section, the term "born alive", with respect to a member of the species homo sapiens, means the complete expulsion or extraction from his or her mother of that member, at any stage of development, who after such expulsion or extraction breathes or has a beating heart, pulsation of the umbilical cord, or definite movement of voluntary muscles, regardless of whether the umbilical cord has been cut, and regardless of whether the expulsion or extraction occurs as a result of natural or induced labor, cesarean section, or induced abortion.
> (c) Nothing in this section shall be construed to affirm, deny, expand, or contract any legal status or legal right applicable to any member of the species homo sapiens at any point prior to being "born alive" as defined in this section.
> (Added Pub. L. 107–207, § 2(a), Aug. 5, 2002, 116 Stat. 926.)
> (Pub. L. 102–484, div. A, title XVII, § 1711, Oct. 23, 1992, 106 Stat. 2581.)

THE LAW TODAY

The US Supreme Court has declared abortion to be a fundamental right guaranteed by the US Constitution. The landmark abortion case Roe v. Wade, decided on January 22, 1973 in favor of abortion rights, remains the law of the land. The 7-2 decision stated that the Constitution gives a guarantee of certain areas or zones of privacy, and that this right of privacy, "is broad enough to encompass a woman's decision whether or not to terminate her pregnancy." The court thoroughly scrutinized the religious and secular history of abortion from the time of the ancient

Greeks. It also found that the opinions and laws relative to abortion had become more restrictive in America as the country matured. It disagreed with this regression. In its decision, it also ruled that under the U.S. Constitution the word 'person' does not include the unborn.

RELIGIOUS ADVOCATES FOR CHANGING THE LAW

The Catholic and Mormon religions have championed purely religious reasons to forbid abortion. Joseph Smith, the founder of the Mormon religion was told by an angel that all souls were created at the time of Adam. (Moses 6:8-9) They must be born so that they can be saved and live in heaven. Jeremiah (1:5) backs up this position. "Before I formed thee in the belly I knew thee; and before thou camest forth out of the womb I sanctified thee, and I ordained thee a prophet unto the nations."

The Catholic position is more complicated. The Bible tells us that Adam and Eve sinned by eating the fruit of the Tree of Knowledge. If Bishop Ussher's calculations are correct, this would have been in 4004 BC. Some early Christian writers believed that this sin was inherited by all of us. Baptism was the way to wash away that sin and start living the good life that can get you to heaven.

Mary, the mother of Jesus, must have been perfect from the beginning. Many theologians believed this, then in 1854, Pope Pius IX declared officially that Mary was conceived without Original Sin—her Immaculate Conception. If she was conceived, that must have been the beginning of life and her soul was obviously in existence when she was conceived. So, life must start at conception for everyone. Consequently, in 1869 the same pope decided that all abortions are immoral since all zygotes and embryos have souls.

CHAPTER FOUR

OPINIONS, FACTS, AND EFFECTIVE THINKING

HOW MUCH DO WE EVALUATE THE ISSUES?

WE BELIEVE WHAT WE HEAR

It is puzzling that 60 years ago the evangelical Bible Belt in the Midwest, and the Republican Party, were leading advocates of abortion, The Democrats and Catholics fought it. Now the tides have changed. It goes to show you that if you can repeat a message enough, that many, or most, people will believe it.

America's very low educational rankings seem to indicate that people will believe what they hear the most often. Those that watch CNN will overwhelmingly have different information than those who watch Fox News. Since we develop our opinions based on what we see and hear, if we hear only one side of an argument, we won't be able to make informed decisions.

Whether this has anything to do with education has been a concern. The latest international education scores (PISA—Program for International Student Assessment) in reading, math, and science shows the U.S. ranking 31st of the 70 countries assessed. The countries that were less religious ranked much higher than the U.S. in their educational knowledge. Perhaps the more educated countries have more citizens who have analyzed the facts and the arguments relative to a creating God and a life after death. Perhaps they are more aware of the tragedies caused by a "merciful" Supernatural. Prayer didn't ease the hurricanes of Texas, Florida, and Puerto Rico. It didn't help ISIS to establish a religious state. It didn't stop the child abuse by Catholic priests and Baptist ministers.

The U.S. has 38% of its citizens believing in the idea that God created the world less than 10,000 years ago. Scientific measurements show that it was over 13 billion years ago that the universe was begun—and the God as Creator hypothesis is not a part of it.

Another fact to consider is that fewer people are needed, especially in the laboring force. In 1900, the life expectancy of men at birth was 47 years. For women, it was 49. Now it is 76 for men and 81 for women. How many people are needed with automation doing nearly all the labor-intensive jobs?

Retirement at 65 or 67 is another factor. In 1936, when Social Security was begun, retirement was at 65 while the life expectancy was 64. The government made money. The government uses the contributions as part of their annual income. While the government officially "borrows" the money, it is a very large part of the U.S. government's $2.5 trillion national debt—the world's largest. The problem is that pensions must be paid with each succeeding budget—and the amount due increases yearly.

People are used to the tradition of retiring in the mid-60s. Their Social Security contributions are used up in 5 to 7 years, but they live another 15. (Life expectancy at birth is near 80, but those who live to 65 can expect another 20.5 years.) The government isn't used to this! So, let's encourage more births and outlaw abortions so that these eventual workers will help to pay for the benefits of those who are retired.

The obvious problem is that if we need 5 to 7 new workers to support a retiree now, we will need 26 to 50 to support those 5 to 7 when they retire in 45 years. Then in another 40 or 50 years we will need another 150 to 250 to support them.

The obvious solutions would be to increase the required payroll taxes that pay for retirement, or raise the retirement age—or both! But in our democratic republic how many legislators would be re-elected if they voted against our traditional retirement expectations? So, let's outlaw abortions to produce more workers!

The major concern we hear the most seems to be—how will we feed them. But perhaps there are other concerns. How will they be educated? Where will the new jobs appear—with robots, computers, 3D printing, and artificial intelligence doing the traditional jobs. One solution might be a world-wide emphasis on contraceptives and abortion. But NO! That would go against our religious and secular traditions!

INTERNATIONAL HUMAN RIGHTS STATEMENTS

National and international organizations have advocated family-planning for a number of years. They have also called for both more freedom and equality in making one's own decisions on how and where to live. These are often antithetical aspirations.

When one has a number of children, such as in Mali where the fertility rate is 7, the status of the mother or father may be enhanced with a large family, or they are praised by their religious leaders. So, reducing the average family size is more than difficult.

RELIGIOUS BELIEFS CAN INTERFERE WITH SOCIAL REALITIES

Just look at the Dugger family in Arkansas. This highly religious family with 19 children, all home-schooled and none college educated, has been praised in America and rewarded with a reality TV show that paid them at least $25,000 per episode until it was cancelled because it was revealed that one of the boys had molested several girls when he was a teenager.

The Biblical command in the Garden of Eden to "be fruitful and multiply and replenish the earth" was issued when there were only two people on earth, Adam and Eve. The question is whether since the earth is now more "replenished" than it has ever been, does that command tell us now to stop replenishing? Is it even possible that multiplying once the earth is replenished a sin because it exceeds God's command?

DECLARATIONS OF HUMAN RIGHTS

Internationally we have some major pronouncements such as the United Nations' 1948 Universal Declaration of Human Rights, and their 1966 International Covenant on Civil and Political Rights. In Europe, we have the European Convention on Human Rights and Fundamental Freedoms. Each guarantees the rights of women. The UN also clearly states that the child has rights after being born. Some women have successfully used these lists of rights in courts to counter religious arguments against abortion.

The European Convention, enforced by the European Court of Justice, has made some decisions regarding equal rights that are not only upsetting to the countries' courts that were overruled, but may play a part in countries considering leaving the EU.

Two such decisions were somewhat influential in the United Kingdom's decision to leave the European Union. The UK wanted to make its own decisions of what was best for them. One such case involved a violent Islamic terrorist that the EU did not want to allow to return. The other involved a murderer who had stomped a man do death because he would not give him a cigarette. While serving his life sentence, he married a female prisoner. They wanted a child, the British courts said "no." One might expect that with two criminal parents, one a sadistic murderer, the child might not have an ideal family life. Along with this, it is highly likely that the child would be raised on the meager welfare payments from the state. But human rights prevail over the needs of a society!

In Africa, the Maputo Protocol (The Protocol to the African Charter on Human and Peoples' Rights on the Rights of Women in Africa) is legally binding on the 37 countries that have ratified it. Included in it is the elimination of genital mutilation and the right to political equality for women. It also allowed abortion "in cases of sexual assault, rape, incest, and where the continued pregnancy endangers the mental and physical health of the mother or the life of the mother or the fetus." A year later, in 2017, African leaders went further, viewing abortion as a human right. There has been opposition by the Catholics to the abortion legalization, and by some Muslim countries to the outlawing of "female circumcision,"

WHAT DO THE LATEST ABORTION LAWS PROTECT?

Human life begins:

➢ Life beginning at conception: Alabama

➢ Life as beginning with the fetal heartbeat, at about six weeks is protected in: Louisiana, Georgia, Ohio, Kentucky, Mississippi

➢ After 8 weeks in: Missouri

- 18 weeks: Utah

Other factors:

- No exception for rape or incest: Louisiana, Missouri, Alabama, Ohio
- Exceptions: life of the mother Louisiana, Alabama, Georgia, Utah
- Severe deformity to child (medically futile): Louisiana
- Parental approval required: Missouri

These laws were passed with generally huge majorities:

- The Louisiana law passed the legislative houses by 79-23 and 31-5 majorities.
- The Missouri law passed 110-44 and 24-10
- The Alabama law passed 74-3 and 25-6
  - Ohio 56-39 and 18-15
  - Utah (Senate vote 23-6)

Some might wonder why this obviously religious anti-abortion idea is not mentioned in the Bible. It is also not against Federal law.

I guess, that if I believe it--it doesn't have to be in the Bible. God obviously forgot to include it.

The Mormons believe that all souls were created with the creation of the world. Plato had believed something like this—there was a pre-existence of one's self and some of what had been learned in a prior life was known when we are born. Origen, one of the early Church fathers believed it also. But in the Second Council of Constantinople, in 553, by a "democratic" vote decided that Origen's ideas were false. The all-knowing prelates chose not to believe Jeremiah. So the idea was lost until Joseph Smith revived it.

PENALTIES FOR THOSE WHO AID IN ABORTIONS

The penalty for doctors who are abortion providers in Alabama is 10 to 99 years in prison. However, the greatest number of abortions, estimated at 20,000 to 30,000 per year, are the spontaneous abortions, also termed miscarriages, that are caused by God.

To be fair, God should be punished at least as stringently as physicians who perform abortions. Since it is useless to subpoena God, perhaps the churches that worship Him should be closed. This would include Catholic, Baptist, and many other such churches. That might make Him think twice!

ANTI-ABORTION LAWS RECENTLY DEFEATED

Delaware and Florida have defeated stronger abortion laws. Other states are passing, or thinking of passing, more lenient abortion laws. Someday the U.S. may equal its neighbor to the north in allowing abortions on demand.

New York allows abortions even if Roe v. Wade is overturned. The vote was 9242 in the Assembly and 38-24 in the Senate.

Vermont and Illinois are considering abortion a fundamental right. Expanded rights to abortion are also being considered in: Rhode Island, Maine, Nevada, and Hawaii.

DOES EDUCATION, OR THE LACK OF IT, PLAY A PART?

We can look for a number of reasons for certain states to embrace the idea of life starting sometime before birth. One is the education level of the state. US News does a number rankings of schools, colleges, and states. Of the 50 states, Alabama ranks last in education, 50th! New Mexico ranks 49th, Louisiana 48th, Alaska 47th (They are considering the harshest abortion law yet devised.) Mississippi is 46th, Arkansas is 42nd, Kentucky is 38th, Ohio 31st, Georgia 30th, and Missouri 27th.

One might wonder if the low levels of educational achievement might be a factor in their not evaluating all of the options in any serious political question.

The US News rankings of state universities is somewhat similar, but some states do somewhat better with their universities, but their tuition levels may prohibit many students from attending. The ranking and tuition levels according to the US News rankings are:

➤ Alabama rankings 115 and 129 ($11,000 in state tuition)

➤ Louisiana 140 ($10,000 to $12,000)

➤ Mississippi 152 ($9,000)

➤ Arkansas 152 (tie) ($9,000)

➤ Ohio 56 ($11,000)

➤ Georgia 46 ($12,000)

➤ Missouri 129 ($10,000)

YOUNG UNEDUCATED MOTHERS IN ALABAMA

Alabama's pregnancy rate per 1,000 girls aged 15-19 is 40.1. And their teen birth rate is 20.7 per 1000 girls. Does this have anything to do with their dismal education performance?

The Alabama pregnancy rate is higher than the U.S. average and its abortion rate is below the U.S. average. So the state has a very high number of very young mothers. We can assume that they are not highly educated. It is conceivable that the children will not grow up in an enriched environment.

WHO IS RIGHT ON THIS ISSUE OF ABORTION?

Matthew 18:18-20 tells us that, "Truly I tell you, whatever you bind on earth will be bound in heaven, and whatever you loose on earth will be loosed in heaven. . . Again, truly I tell you that if two of you on earth agree about anything they ask for, it will be done for them by my Father in heaven. For where two or three gather in my name, there am I with them."

So, if two or three Christians agree on an issue, God will accept it. Therefore, both advocating and prohibiting abortions are approved by God—as long as the proponents on both sides are Christians. This is necessary because God forgot to mention this practice specifically in His Bible.

IT IS ABOUT TRADITION

By the beginning of the 20th century, abortion was illegal or severely restricted in most countries. The restrictions were either from common law, as in the UK and its possessions, civil law as in other European countries and their possessions, or Islamic law, which was used by some Islamic countries. Where it was outlawed, it was usually because of: danger to the mother from unlicensed abortionists; it was a sin and the laws were geared to punish the sinner; or often, the life of the fetus was considered important.

BUT NEW LAWS CHANGE OUR TRADITIONS

While abortion was criminalized in England in 1861, it was modified in 1967 and in 1990. Ireland had a very restrictive policy, seeing the same value of life of the mother as that of the fetus. But as of 2019, after a referendum, abortion is now allowed in a number of situations.

Today abortion is legally permitted to save the life of the woman in 98% of world's countries. 63% of countries allow it to preserve the physical or mental health of the woman. 43% allow it in the case of rape or incest. 39% allow it if the infant is to be severely impaired. 33% allow abortion for economic or social reasons. 27% allow it when requested by the woman. The developing countries are much less likely to allow abortions than are the developed countries.

But now abortion methods have become incredibly safe, if done by competent people.

In recent decades in Latin America, a combination of legislation and judicial review has lessened the restrictions to abortion.

CHAPTER FIVE

POSITIVES FOR SOCIETY

There are a several major reasons for society to allow or even encourage abortions. One is to be able to limit populations that are overcrowded. Another is to protect children from being born into homes that don't want them. The financial cost to society of unwanted children goes beyond the normal societal expenses of educating their young future citizens, it often includes expenses for orphanages, increased expenses for rehabilitation from physical and mental abuse, drug rehabilitation, and increased expenses for police, judicial procedures, and prisons. (Federal prisons cost $35,000 per year per prisoner. This compares with $70,000 in California and New York and $15,000 in Alabama.) So, if people want lower taxes, abortion is a major way to reduce them.

We now know, from epigenetic research, that abused and neglected children often have changes to their genes and brains that increase their likelihood of becoming violent. Irregularities in the brain's pre-frontal cortex, or areas around the hypothalamus (such as the limbic system or amygdala) can predict violence.

The MAOA (the so-called warrior gene) is one of more than 50 genes that can be influenced epigenetically. The behavioral changes can range from problems with impulse control to the inability to control violent behavior. A classic study in Finland found that such epigenetic residues were found only in violent prisoners, not in the non-violent ones. As a result of the study, it was predicted that 5 to 10% of violent crime in Finland was a result of genetic and epigenetic causes.

Brain research continues to uncover causes of behavior that are related to epigenetic changes. For example, recent research has found that at least one cause of autism is caused by first trimester epigenetic changes to the MEMO1 gene on the second chromosome. Epilepsy can also be influenced by this gene which is responsible for the development of important brain cells.

This is also true of neurotransmitter activity--with increases of dopamine or decreases in serotonin. These changes begin in the intra-uterine environment and accumulate through life if stresses persist. Such stresses can include: a pregnant mother who is unhappy, or on legal and illegal drugs. After birth, the child's negative epigenetic changes an come from being bullied, being neglected, physical or sexual abuse, etc.

A society might require that fetuses which are likely to be unloved, abused, or neglected be aborted. The costs of the potentially unloved children in terms of societal problems range well beyond the financial.

FINANCIAL REASONS

Abortion reduces welfare costs to taxpayers. The Congressional Budget Office evaluated a proposed anti-abortion bill that would ban all abortions nationwide after 20 weeks of pregnancy, and found that the resulting additional births would increase the federal deficit by $225 million over nine years--due to the increased need for Medicaid coverage. Also, since many women seeking late-term abortions are economically disadvantaged, their children are likely to require welfare assistance.

Every child, wanted or unwanted, costs about $120,000 if they go to public schools. Then there are the significant police, judicial, and prison expenses for those who go wrong. The average cost of incarcerating a juvenile who has run afoul of the law is $112,000 per year.

The cost of an abortion can be free for impoverished women from some clinics, such as Planned Parenthood. Other physician performed procedures usually cost between $300 during the first trimester to $3,000 during the second trimester. Most are paid by the woman, but even if the government paid for them all, it would be far ahead financially since it would not have to pay the education or other expenses that many children and adults require of the government.

Then there is the probable economic advantage that if the women who did not want children were to stay in the work force or in higher education, the society would profit--especially if they work at the higher-level jobs.

TAXATION

While the U.S. has a relatively low taxation rate, by developed country standards (about 28% for all taxes, compared with the 40+% in Europe), the citizenry continually complains about their high taxes. Allowing for abortions will substantially reduce the need for taxes in many areas, such as: education, Medicaid, prisons, police, welfare, etc.) For example:

In 2015, Alabama had 5900 legal abortions

Georgia 2000

Ohio 21000

Missouri 4800

Louisiana 9400

Texas 54,000

Utah 3,000

The education tax dollars saved in these 7 states for 2015 totaled $12 billion. Texas saved $650,000,000 in education expenses, in 2017, from the abortions performed.

For the 638,000 abortions performed in the U.S. that year, the savings in primary and secondary education dollars was in excess of $76 billion. This would be enough to give every one of the 20 million college students $3800 every year. Or if based on need, far more than that for the poorer students.

THE WORLD IS OVERPOPULATED

Every child, wanted or unwanted, contributes to the world's overpopulation. Overpopulation is the planet's major problem. It is responsible for climate change and many other societal problems, like wars and terrorism, plastics in the ocean, over-fishing, garbage disposal problems, the lack of potable water, and a host of other problems.

The population now is over seven and a half billion people, most of whom live in the cities. According to Professor Emeritus David Pimentel, of Cornell

University—the major authority on overpopulation, if all people are to live at the same standards as found in the developed countries in the West, one to one and a half billion would be the planet's maximum capacity.

City living is usually accompanied by the greater use of concrete for buildings and roads. Concrete production produces 5 to 8% of CO_2 emissions—second only to fossil fuel burning. Concrete and asphalt in buildings and roads often cover topsoil that is necessary for growing crops, so agriculture is impaired. Then when rains come, since there is less ground to absorb the water, heavy runoff or floods carry away some of the topsoil. Dr. Pimentel believes that this soil erosion is the second biggest problem for our world—after overpopulation.

FEWER PEOPLE WILL REDUCE THE GREENHOUSE GASES THAT CREATE GLOBAL WARMING AND CLIMATE CHANGE

The average person in a developed country adds about 5,000 tons of carbon dioxide to the atmosphere. To this is added methane and other greenhouse gases that result from living in an advanced society. If the person eats beef, other meats, or eggs—or drinks milk—much more methane is added to the atmosphere. And methane is more damaging than carbon dioxide. Additionally, the progeny of that unwanted child will each contribute to the problem.

According to the United Nations, in the last twenty years, 91% of natural disasters were caused by climate change, due to greenhouse gases. These disasters include: wildfires, droughts, floods, hurricanes, tornadoes, heat waves, famines, and excessive rain and snow storms. The cost of these was $2.25 trillion.

FEWER PEOPLE EASES THE NEED FOR FRESH WATER FOR PERSONAL NEEDS AND FOOD PRODUCTION

There is a great deal of water on the earth—most of it is unusable salt water. Some of the fresh water is frozen in ice sheets and glaciers. Much of fresh water is not potable (drinkable). Only about 0.003% of water is potable. Much of that is used in agriculture.

Both non-potable fresh water and sea water can be made drinkable—but it is very expensive. Some cities, like Los Angeles, are working on making sewage water potable. Los Angeles County has some areas where they use "gray water" (partially treated water) in some agricultural situations.

FREEDOM FOR THE CITIZENS TO CHOSE THE WAY TO LIVE THEIR LIVES

The Roe v. Wade decision affirmed this freedom as Constitutionally required. But some pseudo-religious people believe that abortion is frowned on by God. The evidence herein presented shows that God even requires abortion in some situations.

REDUCTION IN CRIME

Abortion reduces crime. According to a study co-written in 2001, by Freakonomics co-author Steven D. Levitt, PhD, of the University of Chicago, and John Donahue of Yale, and published in the peer-reviewed Quarterly Journal of Economics, legalized abortion has contributed significantly to recent crime reductions. About 18 years after abortion was legalized, crime rates dropped significantly. It was also found that crime rates dropped earlier in states that had previously allowed abortion. Poorer women in areas of high crime rates might also be quite likely to avail themselves of abortion.

Studies in Canada and Australia found the same thing. Some critics mention that the drop in crack cocaine use or better policing techniques might also explain the findings. But these uncorroborated ideas have also been criticized.

SEPARATION OF CHURCH AND STATE

It seems that even when we have the theoretical separation between church and state, the church's theology may remain in the minds of the judges and legislators. Even atheists often carry religious assumptions with them from childhood or from the community. But fetuses have not always been so protected.

Historically, late term fetuses, or even infants, have not escaped the possibility that they won't see tomorrow. Subsistence economies often can't provide for every "product of passion" that pops into their financially limited world. Some societies see no need to nurture those infants who are unlikely to strongly wield a scythe or a sword for several years. When the physical is more important than the spiritual, any manner of eugenic devices may be allowed or encouraged. Therefore, infanticide has often been the necessary action. Luckily, today, contraception and abortion are more generally available—and are certainly preferable to killing a newborn. But as we know, unwanted babies often are found in trash cans.

Whatever the issue—abortion, gun control, free speech, marijuana legalization, climate change, or any of the pressing issues for American and the world—we must look to facts and logic for the best chance at understanding the problem and solving it. Mere opinions, based on traditions or wishes, murky that waters that must be clear.

Legislators, judges, and the rest of us, are often tethered to traditions or imprisoned by our opinions. And we are often influenced by the loudest voice in the room.

OUR FREEDOM OF SPEECH IDEAS

For example, in the freedom of speech area, the original intent was to allow the expression of well thought-out political opinions, no matter how contrary they might be to prevailing thought. Our Supreme Court has limited such speech during wartime and for communists advocating the overthrow of the government. And, God knows that the Founding Fathers had no intention to violently overthrow the government of King George!

But the Court in Brandenburg v. Ohio, in 1969, astonished a few people. At a Ku Klux Klan meeting in Brandenburg, rural Ohio, one of the speeches referred to "revengeance" against "niggers", "Jews", and those who supported them. (If "revengeance" doesn't sound like a word to you, it really isn't—but you can believe that it has a powerful meaning to some uneducated white Christians with huge inferiority feelings. And the mantra that "we is better than them," is an easy way to develop the feeling of power that insecure people need.)

The Court changed its emphasis on what is not allowed as free speech from being "a bad tendency," as in its earlier cases to an "imminent lawless action, that is likely to incite and produce such lawless action." So it would appear that as long as you don't say "let's kill them NOW," and leave it to the audience as to whether killing them tomorrow will be soon enough, it appears that your speech is protected!

AND GUN CONTROL

Similarly, the recent change in the Second Amendment's original meaning of "A well-regulated militia being necessary, the right to bear arms shall not be infringed," has had its original meaning changed both philosophically and grammatically by the Court.

So, while the right to own guns, for most people, is the law of the land, it has only been true since the decisions made in 2008 and 2010. One might suspect that the writers of the Constitution would disagree with the recent court decisions—at least if we can believe Founding Father James Madison's essay in Federalist Papers, Number 46. He tells us of the intention of the "right to bear arms" phrase. It was all about a national guard to protect the nation. It wasn't about hunting or self-defense. But why are we paying Supreme Court Justices if it isn't to change the meaning of the Constitution? At least it keeps them off the welfare rolls!

AND BACK TO ABORTION

There are no religious or societal reasons for not applauding the abortions of unwanted children. The opposition to abortions comes from:

➢ Religious sects that want more members,

➢ Business people who want more customers,

➢ Politicians who want more soldiers, and

➢ People who want to continue their local traditions.

These desires are generally couched in religious suppositions that may, or may not, be based on their scriptures. But even if based on scriptures, rather than facts—they are in the areas of the non-provable—that is why "faith" is essential. And it seems that in America, faith is generally more important than facts. The legislators and courts generally bend over backwards to protect opinions, or beliefs, no matter how anti-social they may be.

DO YOU THINK THAT FACTS, RATHER THAN FAITH, MIGHT BE THE BASES OF BETTER LAWS AND COURT DECISIONS?

APPENDIX A   ABORTION INFORMATION

Many readers have expressed an interest in exploring the possibilities for abortion services for themselves or others. Having a child certainly is a major emotional, time, and financial consideration. Certainly, the parents' needs and desires, as well as the needs of the child must be paramount.

Some states have simple requirements for abortion, as does Canada. Some states make it difficult to obtain one. However, if you do not want to become a parent within the year, travelling to a nearby state for an abortion, whatever the cost, will save you over $200,000, according to the U.S. Government.

The information on the following site is important to read to get general information on abortion. It does not cover some of the long-term considerations.

If you are reading an e-book version and are connected to the Internet, merely click the link. If you are reading a print book, write the following link address into the address bar on your device.

https://www.plannedparenthood.org/

Important considerations for those considering an abortion. And, how to get an in-clinic abortion.

https://www.plannedparenthood.org/learn/abortion/in-clinic-abortion-procedures/how-do-i-get-an-in-clinic-abortion

Canada has the world's most lenient abortion laws. This site may be of interest.

http://www.nafcanada.org/hotline.html

There are a number of international groups that can aid those seeking to end a pregnancy. The International Federation of Professional Abortion and Contraception Associations may be of service.

https://fiapac.org/en/links/3/

INDEX

SYMBOLS
3D printing, 6, 11, 17

A
Abortion, 1–8, 11–25, 27–29
Abortion laws, 3, 18, 20
Abused, 2, 23–24
Alabama, 3, 18–21, 23, 25
Alaska, 20
Artificial intelligence, 6, 11, 17
Autism, 23

B
Bathsheba, 9
Beliefs, 3, 5, 7, 17, 29
Bible, 3, 5, 7–11, 14–15, 19, 21
Business, 29

C
California, 23
Catholic, 7, 14–15, 18–19
CNN, 15
CO2, 26
Colleges, 20
Crime, 4, 9, 23, 27

D
David, 9, 25
Deuteronomy, 8–9

E

Education, 2–3, 5–6, 15, 20–21, 24–25
Ephesians, 10
European court, 18
Evangelical, 7, 15
Exodus, 8, 10

F

Fox News, 15
Freakonomics, 27

G

Georgia, 18–20, 25

H

Hammurabi, 6
Hosea, 8

J

Jeremiah, 7, 9, 14, 19
Judicial, 2, 22–24

L

Leviticus, 9–11
Life expectancy, 6, 16
Louisiana, 18–20, 25

M

Maputo, 18
Matthew, 8, 21
Medicaid, 2, 24–25
MEMO1 gene, 23
Methane, 26
Mississippi, 18, 20
Missouri, 18–20, 25
Mormon, 7, 14, 19
Moses, 6–8, 14

N

Nation, 10, 14, 17, 26, 29
New Testament, 10
New York, 20, 23
Numbers, 7

O

Old Testament, 8
Overpopulation, 2–3, 16, 25–26

P

Person, 3–4, 7–11
PISA, 15
Pregnancy, 13, 18, 21, 24
Pregnancy rate, 21
prison, 2, 19, 24
prisons, 23, 25
punishment, 3, 8, 11

R

Rankings, 15, 20
Reason, 2–3, 6, 14, 20, 22–24, 29
Robotics, 6

S

Samuel, 9
Scandinavian, 5
Scriptures, 5, 29
Second trimester, 24
Separation of church and state, 4, 11, 27
Slavery, 3, 9–11
Social Security, 16

T

Taxation, 3, 25

Terrorist, 18
Timothy, 10
Titus, 10
Traditions, 3, 5–6, 17, 21, 28–29

U

Universal Declaration of Human Rights, 17
Universities, 6, 20

W

Warrior gene, 23
Water, 2, 4, 7–8, 25–28
Welfare, 2, 18, 24–25, 29